A Retreat
in the Desert
with Jesus
A Lenten Survival Kit

JESUS: OUR EXEMPLAR — During His agony in the Garden of Gethsemane (and later just before His Death on the Cross), Jesus entrusted Himself to the Heavenly Father in prayer. We should do the same.

A RETREAT
IN THE DESERT
WITH JESUS
A LENTEN SURVIVAL KIT

By

Bernard-Marie, O.F.S.

Translated from the French by
Rev. Msgr. C. Anthony Ziccardi, S.S.L., S.T.D.

CATHOLIC BOOK PUBLISHING CORP.
New Jersey

NIHIL OBSTAT: Rev. Pawel Tomczyk, Ph.D.
Censor Librorum

IMPRIMATUR: ✠ Most Rev. Kevin J. Sweeney, D. D.
Bishop of Paterson

September 8, 2020

This book was originally published in French by Editions Mame, Paris, 2016 under the title *La Carême des humbles: Retraite au désért avec Jésus.*

(T-936)

ISBN 978-1-947070-89-9
20 MG 1
© 2020 by Catholic Book Publishing Corp.
77 West End Rd.
Totowa, NJ 07512
Printed in the U.S.A.
catholicbookpublishing.com

CONTENTS

INTRODUCTION

Understanding Lent better

The Christian life can be defined as a life of faith, hope, and love with Christ and in His Spirit. The Apostle Paul captured this reality by a single exclamation: "It is no longer I who live, but Christ who lives in me!" (Gal 2:20)

To live better this divine companionship, the Church invites the faithful to walk in the footsteps of Christ. He understands them better than they do themselves because He has preceded them on the earthly journey. Through all kinds of joyful and sorrowful events, He has blazed for them the trail of salvation on earth and of eternal happiness in the hereafter. Thus, after their baptism, believers are invited to relive, most notably by the liturgical cycle, the great mysteries of the life of their Lord. With Him, this entails being born from above (Jn 3:3) and sharing in His struggle against the evil powers, in His ministry of preaching and consolation for the suffering, and in His sacrifice of love for all humanity by accepting "each day" (Lk 9:23) to carry one's own cross behind Him.

Certainly, the liturgical year is one particularly beautiful and fruitful way to follow Christ in His various mysteries. This time of grace starts with the season of Advent followed closely by Christmas. Then follows the time of preparation for the great Passion and paschal Resurrection. It is the time of Lent or Forty (*quadragesima*), this is to say, the period of forty days during which "Jesus was led by the Spirit into the desert to be tempted by the devil" (Mt 4:1). The use of Forty or *Quadriges-ima* is not accidental. It matches the forty-year trek of the Hebrews in the desert of Sinai towards the Promised Land. This number of forty days begins with Ash Wednesday and goes to Holy Saturday evening, the vigil of Easter, and it does not include any Sunday in this period; for, liturgically, Sundays are always considered a joyous celebration of the victory over evil without prescribed penitential concern. Our countdown of the days takes into account this aspect and concludes with the joyous day of Easter, which is thus envisioned as the first day of the New Time. It has seemed natural to us to conclude our spiritual journey with this day following Lent because it is this day that gives meaning to the rest, that illumines all, that gives the noticeable clarity of eternity and supernatural peace to the period of desert and privation which has preceded it.

How to proceed practically

Our goal here is daily to offer the reader various pathways of reflection in order to facilitate prayer, love, and action in the directions that the Church herself is moving at the same time in her liturgy. We first quote a brief scriptural excerpt from that day's liturgy. It is this biblical passage that establishes the subject for the day as well as its tenor. This is one of the characteristics of this project that determines other aspects of it. The official liturgical translation has the merit of being well suited to public proclamation and to simple understanding of the text, but other translations are not less rich. [In this English translation, we will be quoting primarily from the *New Catholic Bible* which is derived from the Hebrew and Greek texts].

After the Scripture and in line with it, we offer a brief reflection borrowed from the Tradition of the Church, from the early or the more recent Tradition.

After the doctrinal instruction, there follows a short reflection by the author who repeats the theme from a spiritual point of view that may include the perspective of final purposes (eschatology).

This time of meditation leads naturally to a practical side: the suggestion of a concrete act of conversion.

Finally, the day ends with a suggested prayer that may be from a saint or from the author.

Consideration before starting

The present work does not have as its purpose to replace the Lenten pathways that are offered by parishes during this important liturgical season. It is more like a survival kit in the desert if one has neglected to bring along any provisions. To the *anawim* of today, to the humble of this time, we offer some primers, some small but rich seeds, with the hope that they will grow and nurture the believer in a sustained fashion. May the believer make the effort to use these each day without going on to the text of the next day in order to benefit better from the grace of each day!

Outside of the actual season of Lent, this book, rich in spiritual primers, could also guide every person desiring to "rest a while" with the Lord (Mk 6:31). It could help them to take stock of their life and thus live better the grace of one's baptism.

Day 1

Ash Wednesday

CONVERTING AND BELIEVING
IN THE GOSPEL

Scripture

"Yet even now, says the Lord, return to me with all your heart, with fasting with weeping, and with mourning. Rend your hearts and not your garments, and turn back to the Lord, your God."

Joel 2:12-13

Church Tradition

Saint John Paul II (20th century):"Conversion of the heart is a gift of God, an initiative on his part. Our faith teaches us that this initiative takes concrete form in the mystery of Christ the redeemer, the reconciler and the liberator of man from sin in all its forms. Let us be reminded always of that *vertical* dimension of division and reconciliation concerning the relationship between man and God. In the vision of faith, the *vertical* dimension always prevails over the *horizontal* dimension, that is to say, over the reality of division between people and the need for reconciliation between them."

Apostolic Exhortation *Reconciliation and Penance*

Brief meditation

In order to follow Jesus more closely, whether that be in the desert period of holy Lent or during the more ordinary times of our lives, let us first recognize our condition: we are sinners. Let us acknowledge sincerely that we do not love as we should and that, in order to become true disciples, we must rediscover a living contact with the grace coming from above, the *vertical* dimension, as John Paul II said. This grace does not come except from the Lord alone, for only He knows us perfectly and wants our true happiness.

Concrete act of conversion

Let us find a quiet place to practice some moments of interior silence. This could be a church, a chapel, somewhere in nature, or a private room in your home (Mt 6:6). For several moments let us think gratefully about the God who created us and who has forgiven us in Christ. Let us ask Him for the strength to live these forty days of Lent with the sentiments that animated the Heart of His Son in the desert. During this time of purification, let us consider making some humble gesture of retreat from the world and of greater attachment to His Kingdom; for example, a fast from food, the sacrifice of a daily cocktail, giving up some TV time for a brief visit with a lonely person.

Prayer

Approve, Lord, the ashes (Job 42:6) of my humble repentance and the sweet scent (Mt 6:17) of my good actions. Thank You for offering me this time of penance in order that I might rediscover the purity of heart that will allow me to see You more clearly in all things (Mt 5:8). Free me from selfishness in order that I may serve You better in the poor and the suffering. Amen.

Day 2
Thursday after Ash Wednesday

DENYING ONESELF

Scripture

"Jesus was saying to all who were with him, 'Anyone who wishes to follow me must deny himself, take up his cross daily, and follow me. For whoever wishes to save his life will lose it, but whoever loses his life for my sake will save it.'"

Luke 9:23-24

Church Tradition

Abba Pambo, father of the desert (4th century): "Four monks of Scetis came one day to see Abba Pambo. Each one entered in his turn and revealed the virtue of his neighbor. The first fasted a great deal; the second practiced almsgiving assiduously; the third helped all whom he met; and they said of the fourth that he had lived for twenty-two years in obedience to an old man. Abba Pambo called together the first three monks and he declared to them: 'I tell you, the virtue of this last one is the greatest. In effect, it is by personal choice that each of you has acquired that virtue that he possesses. But he, restraining his own will, does the will of another. Now it is just such men who become martyrs if they persevere to the end.'"

Sayings of the Fathers, Recension of Pelagius and John, Pambo, 3

Brief meditation

To decide one fine day to deny yourself in order to imitate the saints is a beautiful initiative, but usually it is too unrewarding or lasting. Christian conversion is not a process of behavioral imitation. We do not easily leave the self behind images of oneself that we prize as a personal idol. We do not manage to free ourselves from our earthly "I" unless we are moved by the powerful attraction of a noble goal, essentially for Another whom we love more than ourselves. Now, what being would merit that we renounce everything for them except Christ who has given everything to humanity including His own life. If we thus focus more on our Savior than ourselves, it is He who will take care of us and tell us who we truly are and what we must do.

Concrete act of conversion

To forget oneself and think more about God and neighbor is a matter of no more than praying and behaving charitably. We must also learn to adore and to give thanks, acknowledging the Creator in wholehearted and loving spontaneity.

Prayer

"Praised be to You, my Lord, with all Your creatures, especially for my lord Brother Sun, who brings the day, who is beautiful and radiant with great splendor. Of You, Most High, he gives testimony."

"Canticle of the Creatures," Saint Francis of Assisi
ms. 338 of Assisi, str. 2

Day 3
Friday after Ash Wednesday

OPENING OURSELVES UP
TO COMPASSION

Scripture

"Thus says the Lord: 'This rather is the type of fast that I wish: to loosen the fetters of injustice, to undo the thongs of the yoke, to set free those who are oppressed and to break every yoke, to share your bread with the hungry and to offer shelter to the homeless poor, to clothe the naked when you behold them and not turn your back on your own kin.'"   *Isaiah 58:6-7*

Church Tradition

Saint John Paul II (20ᵗʰ century): "We should all give witness concretely to the mercy of God. For this, a new *creativity in charity* is needed. May this creativity never be lacking when a needy person pleads: 'Blessed are the merciful, for they shall obtain mercy' (Mt 5:7)."

Homily for the Beatification of Jan Beyzym
August 18, 2002

Brief meditation

Praying is a type of work—the spending of energy for love of Love. But giving witness *concretely* of the mercy of the Lord who has made His home in us (Jn 14:23) is also a work, a duty, a mission deriving from above and from our inner selves where the Spirit of Christ dwells (Gal 4:6). Consequently, loving *concretely* means not only praying for the hungry but also sharing with them some of our bread, not only sending a financial contribution to a humanitarian agency but also offering some of our time to seek out the lonely who are too hopeless to complain or plead.

Concrete act of conversion

Especially this Friday, in memory of the Crucified One, let us practice a light fast that is secret and smart. Let us eat a little less and drink a little more water than usual, which will in no way harm our health. Let us try to smile at someone we meet casually, even and especially if we ourselves are in a gloomy mood.

Prayer

"God, merciful Father, in Your Son, Jesus Christ, You have revealed Your love and poured it out upon us in the Holy Spirit, the Comforter. We entrust to You today the destiny of the world and of every man and woman. Bend down to us sinners, heal our weakness, conquer all evil, and grant that all the peoples of the earth may experience Your mercy. In You, the Triune God, may they ever find the source of hope. Eternal Father, by the Passion and Resurrection of Your Son, have mercy on us and upon the whole world! Amen."

Act of Consecration of the World to the Divine Mercy
St. John Paul II, Krakow, August 17, 2002

Day 4
Saturday after Ash Wednesday

RECOGNIZING OUR OWN WRETCHEDNESS

Scripture

"Jesus said to them in reply: 'It is not the healthy who need a physician, but rather those who are sick. I have not come to call the righteous but sinners to repentance.'" *Luke 5:31-32*

Church Tradition

Blessed Columba Marmion (19th-20th centuries.): "It is not our perfections that attract God to us, Him Who is encircled by myriads of angels. Rather, it is our wretchedness and destitution confessed before His mercy. The greater is our poverty the more the ineffable riches of Christ find their place in us. Our wretchedness, known and confessed, calls forth His bounty."

Marmion Collection, specifically *Union with God*

Brief meditation

If we can canonically have recourse to the Sacrament of Reconciliation, it would be good to consider doing so during Lent. If we have nothing or little to accuse ourselves of in confession, then indubitably our conscience has fallen asleep, especially for lack of an active spiritual quest. Even if we have not formally broken God's commandments, there are situations in which we could have done more or better, or perhaps we should have reacted differently and, in any case, not have chosen indifference or inaction. This is called the sin of omission—one of the more frequent yet unrecognized sins.

Concrete act of conversion

Set aside some moments before going to bed to undertake a serious examination of conscience. Let us examine our lives by trying to see ourselves under the glance of Christ. With Him and in the light of the requirements of the gospel, let us see our faults, our errors, and our lack of attention as regards God, our neighbor, and every creature.

Prayer

O Mary, conceived without sin, pray for me who am a sinner. Obtain for me from God perfect contrition and a pure heart. Bring Him the offering of my good intention. May His reign of love come into me and over our world which has great need of it. Amen.

First Sunday of Lent

THE SPIRITUAL BATTLE

Scripture

"Filled with the Holy Spirit, Jesus returned from the Jordan and was led by the Spirit into the desert for forty days, where he was tempted by the devil. During that time he ate nothing, and at the end of it he was famished."

Luke 4:1-2

Church Tradition

Saint Paul VI (20th century): "Not every sin is directly due to diabolical action; nonetheless, it is true that those who do not keep watch over themselves with a certain moral rigor are exposed to the influence of the 'mystery of iniquity' cited by Saint Paul [2 Thes 2:7].... The Christian must be vigilant and strong. He must at times make use of special ascetical practices to escape from certain diabolical attacks. Jesus teaches us this and points to 'prayer and fasting' as the remedy" (Mk 9:29).

General Audience of November 15, 1972

Brief meditation

Venerable Francis Libermann (19th century), who was not lacking a sense of humor, acknowledged that mortification could be a good thing, but it did not oblige us "to mortify others." He also added this advice that sheds light on the sometimes painful mystery of the spiritual battle: "The spirit of mortification should never touch on what is necessary and useful for keeping the body vital" (*Spiritual Letters*, vol. 2, p. 499). Pruning a tree does not mean cutting it into two or depriving it of sunlight or frequent watering or loving care as a parable of Christ invites us to do: "Do not cut down this fig tree. Let it alone for one more year while I dig around it and fertilize it. Perhaps it will bear fruit next year" (Lk 13:8-9).

Concrete act of conversion

Above all, it is the patience of love that strengthens the soul and obtains for it the priceless grace of perseverance. Therefore, let us exercise this virtue by making use of the many small disappointments that punctuate our days.

Prayer

"Most gentle Lord Jesus, this trial of today, this difficulty, this sorrow, and this temptation that I have suffered, I offer them to You in union with all that You have endured for me; I offer them for the glory of Your Name and for the salvation of all. Amen."

Louis de Blois (12th century)

Day 5
Monday of the First Week of Lent

SERVING JESUS IN THE POOR

Scripture

"And the King will answer, 'Amen, I say to you, whatever you did for one of the least of these brethren of mine, you did for me.'"

Matthew 25:40

Church Tradition

Saint Isaac the Syrian (7th century): "What is a charitable heart? It is a heart that burns with love for all creation, for people, for birds, for animals, for demons, for all creatures... so great is the compassion that burns without measure in a heart in the image of God."

Spiritual Works, homily 81

Brief meditation

To know and love God is all one (Jn 17:3). We cannot discover Divine Love without at the same time feeling ourselves drawn, carried, embraced by a mysterious fire, in which the emotional element is never the essential aspect. It makes you love as God loves in Spirit and Truth. This Love is universal and leads you to love all creatures, especially the poorest, for love of God. This is why "whoever does not love the brother whom he sees cannot love God whom he does not see" (1 Jn 4:20). Tangible and gratuitous love of one's neighbor is the touchstone of love for the invisible God (Mt 25:40).

The one is the proof of the other. The one can stimulate the other for it is the same love from above that flows among beings that fraternally love each other and their heavenly Father.

Concrete act of conversion

Let us think of the poor people whom we know. What have we done concretely to help them recently? Let us choose to do a charitable deed within the range of what is possible for us and let us accomplish it without delay, a deed as private as possible, a deed that respects the dignity of the person who is helped by us.

Prayer

Lord Jesus, who did not have "a stone" on which to rest Your head (Mt 8:20), grant me the grace to be able to help You soon in a poor person. Amen.

Day 6

Tuesday of the First Week of Lent

PRAYING WITH FEW WORDS AND FORGIVING GENEROUSLY

Scripture

Jesus said to them: "When you pray do not go on babbling endlessly as the pagans do"... "If you forgive others for the wrongs they have done, your heavenly Father will also forgive you."   *Matthew 6:7, 14*

Church Tradition

Father Pius Régamey, O.P. (20th century): "On the practical level, what every believer needs is a prayer formula that they can repeat silently and slowly. It needs to be extremely simple and brief. It must be rich in meaning for the one who has recourse to it, with a significance truly essential to them. For example, 'Jesus, I love you. Come to my aid!' Or 'My God, have mercy on us sinners!'"   *The Spiritual Life, 93*

Brief meditation

Ejaculatory prayer, or the brief invocation shot at God like an arrow, has always existed in the spiritual life as a salutary practice. Christ himself made use of such in Gethsemane: "Abba...not what I want, but what You want" (Mk 14:36). In his private prayer, the hermit Macarius loved to repeat: "As You want and as You know: have mercy!" In the middle of the night, the young Francis of Assisi would

22

not cease to exclaim: "My God and my all!" As he kept vigil, Saint Dominic did not stop repeating: "My God, my Mercy, what is to become of sinners?" The dying Jeanne Jugan was heard to say: "Eternal Father, open Your doors to the most wretched of Your daughters who desires greatly to see You." On her deathbed, Bernadette of Lourdes exclaimed: "Holy Mary, Mother of God, pray for me, poor sinner, poor sinner!" And Thérèse of the Child Jesus said: "My God, I love You!" Mother Teresa liked to repeat: "Lord, give me those who are poor or lonely. Make me a saint according to Your Heart that is gentle and humble!" Let us not doubt, then, that our most beautiful prayers are chiefly pure outbursts of the heart followed by silence.

Concrete act of conversion

After invoking the Holy Spirit, let us ask God to suggest to us a short phrase that could become our ejaculatory prayer for the day or longer.

Prayer

"Lord Jesus, Son of God the Savior, have mercy on me a sinner!"

Eastern Christian formulation of the prayer
of the heart called "The Prayer of Jesus"

Day 7

Wednesday of the First Week of Lent

LEARNING TO ADMIT THAT
WE ARE SINNERS

Scripture

"When God saw by their actions that they had turned from their evil ways, he relented and did not inflict upon them the punishment that he had threatened." *Jonah 3:10*

Church Tradition

Pope Francis (21ˢᵗ century): "All of us are masters of self-justification: No, it's not my fault. In any case, it is not too serious, etc. All of us have good alibis to explain away our infractions and sins. Insisting on our innocence, we no longer make progress in the Christian life.... When we begin to consider seriously what (evil) we are capable of doing, at first we feel bad and are even filled with loathing. Afterwards, our repentance in the Lord's sight brings us peace and salvation. If we do not try to take this first step, then we shall make no progress whatever on the path of the Christian and spiritual life." On Vatican Radio, March 2, 2015

Brief meditation

Too lax an understanding of Anglo-Saxon positive thought has relegated to the realm of the forgotten the Christian sense of failure and its attendant desire to make reparation, and thus also the frequent practice of the Sacrament of Reconciliation. Already in the 1970s, Marthe Robin claimed that the psychotherapist had replaced the confessor and the spiritual director. Perhaps the time has come to return to the right practice of spiritual coaching. Charles de Foucauld held it in great esteem, but under certain conditions: "The priest, in communion with the holy Church and equipped with her powers, is, when he hears confessions and directs souls, one of those to whom Jesus said, 'Whoever listens to you, listens to me'" (Lk 10:16, quoted in the *Directoire* [*Directory*]). One of his first disciples, Father Albert Peyriguère, clarified usefully: "The spiritual director must not put himself between the soul and God, but merely walk behind her (the soul) in such manner that she has in front of her only God. From behind, he (the spiritual director) is there only to motivate and to warn of possible unperceived dangers, certainly not to choose the path in place of his directee."

Concrete act of conversion

If I were to go to confession tomorrow, what would I tell the priest? What resolution would I be ready to make in order to confront better my greatest weakness?

Prayer

"Have mercy upon me, Lord. Help me to be ashamed of myself and grant me Your mercy. Thus, I will be able to be merciful towards others. Amen."

Pope Francis, homily in Saint Martha for Lent,
March 2, 2015

Day 8
Thursday of the First Week of Lent

LOVING ONE'S NEIGHBOR AS ONESELF

Scripture

Jesus said to them: "In everything, deal with others as you would like them to deal with you. This is the Law and the Prophets."

Matthew 7:12

Church Tradition

Saint Thomas Aquinas (13th century): "In itself and in its essence, the perfection of the Christian life consists in charity, which is firstly and principally love of God, and later and as a result (it is) love of neighbor."

Toward the Perfection of the Spiritual Life,
pamphlet 8, 1, § 2

Brief meditation

The fruitful practice of fraternal charity requires discernment. Great carefulness is required in order to give the other what is truly good for him, which may not necessarily consist of material aid or a good word. In this matter, as in the rest, we must imitate God: our justice and our charity must work together to avoid the pain of harshness from our employing too much rigor or the mildness that comes from attending only to the emotions of the present moment. Father Guillaume Pouget (19th century) said this emphatically when he spoke this sentence to his young friend Jean Guitton: "It is no use to be charitable if at first one is not just or to be pious if one does not live out the duties of one's state in life"(*Portrait of M. Pouget*, Jean Guitton).

Concrete act of conversion

Saint Francis de Sales recalled that we must not forget to be charitable towards ourselves. It is not a matter of pampering ourselves, but of being gentle and humble with ourselves as the Lord is with us (Mt 11:29). Thus, in a world of great tensions, it is good to know how to "come away"(Mk 6:31) in order to renew one's physical and spiritual strength.

Prayer

"Lord, grant me to be helpful without imposing myself in order that I may assist others without humiliating them. Make me small and poor enough in order that I myself may be helped by others."

Saint Vincent de Paul (1581-1660)

Day 9
Friday of the First Week of Lent

THE PRIORITY OF INDIVIDUAL FORGIVENESS OVER PUBLIC WORSHIP

Scripture

Jesus said to them: "When offering your gift at the altar, if you should remember that your brother has something against you, leave your gift there at the altar and first go to be reconciled with your brother. Then return and offer your gift."

Matthew 5:23-24

Church Tradition

Nicholas Kabasilas (14th century): "The one who holds a grudge derives no benefit from the Eucharist. Therefore, let us withstand any stirring of anger and let us keep our soul untainted by hatred. The blood of Christ, which was spilled for our reconciliation, does not profit him who is a slave of anger and hatred. Let us have recourse to the priests to confess our sins and taste this purifying blood!"

Life in Christ, VI, 10

Brief meditation

The forgiveness lived by us on earth cannot be mere forgetfulness as though nothing ever happened, as though the wounds of yesteryear completely ceased to hurt. Rather, it is healthy and prudent to keep track of the past, but "with a purified glance" (E. Levinas). Forgiving as Christ did from His cross (Lk 23:34) is to let the persecutor come under a new glance; it is to give him no longer the look of condemnation but of compassion and possible redemption if he decides in turn to love rather than hate.

Concrete act of conversion

Do I have enemies, persons who rightly or wrongly have it in for me? If so, what can I do to make a gesture of reconciliation towards them or at least of appeasement? And then will I not have against me at the very least the Enemy of Christ, since, according to the assurance of Scripture, "Persecution will afflict all who want to live a godly life in Christ Jesus" (2 Tim 3:12).

Prayer

"Lord, when You will come in Your glory, do not recall only men of good will, but also men of bad will.... Grant, Lord, that the fruits we have brought forth may one day be useful for their redemption."

The prayer of a man deported to Buchenwald scrawled on some wrapping paper near a gas chamber

Day 10
Saturday of the First Week of Lent

RETURNING GOOD FOR EVIL

Scripture

Jesus said to them: "Love your enemies, *bless those who curse you, do good to those who slander you,* pray for those who persecute you... Therefore, be perfect as your heavenly Father is perfect." *Matthew 5:44, 48*

here with the addition in Codex Bezae, the Vulgate, and the Peshitta, compare it with *Luke 6:27-28, 36*

Church Tradition

Pastor Richard Wurmbrand (20th century): "To be Christian is to be in Hebrew a *'ani hu'* [cf. Isa 48:12], an *'I-he,'* a human soul in close union with Christ. Thus, to one who has known him for a long time, the Christian can say: 'He who has seen me has seen the Christ' (cf. Jn 14:9)." *Sermons from the Dungeon*

Brief meditation

We should pray as much for the perseverance of the great saints as for the conversion of the most hardened sinners. Some people, these latter ones, are slaves of their sins and of the Evil One; therefore, they deserve our frequent intercessions on their behalf. But the saints most united to Christ, by virtue of their attentive and generous response to God's grace, convert a great number of people (cf. Jas 5:16).

Thus, it is principally against them that the demons come together to focus their attacks. They strive to make them stumble or at least to distract them by pious and noble means that temporarily weaken their judgment and their power of intercession.

Concrete act of conversion

We might try to follow the advice of Blessed Charles de Foucauld: "Among the saints we find most charming, let us choose one who seems to us to have best loved and imitated Jesus Christ. Let us make him [her], then, our very close friend. Let us put ourselves in some fashion under his [her] direction" (*Spiritual Works*).

Prayer

O Mary, compassionate Mother of God, how men brutally treated Your Son during His Passion! How much they hated His cause! How they repaid Him evil for good! With Him forgive them, and forgive us these sins of ignorance and ingratitude, and hasten the coming (Mt 24:22) of His blessed Reign. Amen.

According to a traditional Polish prayer

Second Sunday of Lent

LISTENING TO THE BELOVED

Scripture

"And while he was praying, the appearance of his face underwent a change, and his clothing became dazzling white....Then a voice came out of the cloud, saying, 'this is my Son, my Chosen One. Listen to him.'" *Luke 9:29, 35*

Church Tradition

Saint Athanasius of Sinai (7th century): "In the Transfiguration the signs of the Kingdom were prefigured, the Crucifixion was announced, the beauty of Heaven was disclosed, the second descent and glorious coming of Christ were revealed. It was on Tabor that the splendor of the just was enveloped by the cloud and that future goods were shown as present. By the cloud that wraps it, this mountain announced the future rapture of the just on the clouds (1 Thes 4:17) and prefigured our future form and our being configured to Christ. This place is nothing less than the House of God and the Gate of Heaven (Gen 28:17) towards which we must hasten as did Jesus who, there and in heaven, is our guide and precursor, and with whom we shall shine, configured to His image, perpetually transfigured and divinized."

Homily on the Transfiguration, § 3, 7

Brief meditation

The mystery of Christ's Transfiguration on Tabor is an essential feast of Eastern Christianity. For these Churches, what happened on Tabor is not only prophetic of the painful "exodus"(Lk 9:31) which Jesus would soon experience in Jerusalem but also a tangible beginning of the great transformation in which, in Christ, the whole of creation will share at the end of time (Rom 8:21). Thus, it is for us Christians, in the heart of Lent, a sign of encouragement along the way, an extra reason for hope, a cause for joy even while our disciples' bodies, in a state of deprivation, are on the deserted mountain.

Concrete act of conversion

In the spirit of the Christians of the East, let us take a moment to pray silently before an icon or the picture of an icon (see p. 87). There are very beautiful icons in some of our churches or on the internet.

Prayer

Lord, it is good to remain here close to You. If You wish, make us enter into Your divine light so that to the extent that our nature is not yet deified (2 Pet 1:4) we might glimpse already something of Your very holy Trinity, the source of all knowledge and eternal blessedness. Amen.

Day 11

Monday of the Second Week of Lent

PATTERNING OURSELVES ON
THE MERCIFUL FATHER

Scripture

Jesus said to the crowd: "Be merciful, just as your Father is merciful....Give, and it will be given to you. A good measure, pressed down, shaken together, and running over, will be poured into your lap. The measure that you use for others will be used to measure you."

Luke 6:36, 38

Church Tradition

Saint John Cassian (4th-5th centuries): "The devil does not eat, he does not drink, and he does not get married; and for all this, this great ascetic, formally speaking, is no less a devil. Therefore, let us always join the secondary elements—fasting, vigils, solitude—to the primary end: purity of the heart, which is charity."

Conferences, I, 7

Brief meditation

We do not go up towards God except by means of the two wings of love and truth or, in the language of the Bible, peace and justice (Ps 85:11). Therefore, Christian mercy does not suppose any indulgence whatever of evil; on the contrary, it supposes a just accounting of it so that it may be conquered by understanding and love. If someone has offended our values or ourselves, our forgiveness does not imply indifference towards the slavery to sin into which the offender has fallen. We must pray for their deliverance from evil and conversion to love, which will begin with a genuine act of repentance and a real desire to atone for the wrong that has been done.

Concrete act of conversion

Let us meditate momentarily on the different exemplary acts of forgiveness with which we are familiar, beginning with that of Jesus on the cross: "Father, forgive them, for they do not know what they are doing!" (Lk 23:34); and that of the deacon Stephen in the final moments of his stoning: "Lord, do not hold this sin against them!" (Acts 7:60).

Prayer

Lord, no one can please You unless they have a pure heart and humble spirit. Grant us the grace of looking more like You Who are "gentle and humble of heart" (Mt 11:29), and do not allow the Enemy of humankind to seduce or ensnare us. Amen.

Day 12

Tuesday of the Second Week of Lent

PREFERRING HUMILITY IN EVERYTHING

Scripture

Jesus said to the crowd: "The greatest among you must be your servant. All those who exalt themselves will be humbled, and all those who humble themselves will be exalted."

Matthew 23:11-12

Church Tradition

Saint Augustine of Hippo (4th-5th centuries): "If I did not possess God, it was because Jesus is humble and I was not. And I did not yet know the lessons that His weakness teaches us."

Confessions, VII, 18

Brief meditation

We must not be mistaken as regards humility. One sort of humility is that which is similar to modesty, as pertains to a type of character or to a philosophy of life. The other sort of humility is a pure gift of God and remains, as such, a mystery. It is characterized by the trusting and thankful welcome of our deep being, created "in the image and likeness of God" (Gen 1:26). As such, we cannot become humble except by discovering ourselves as known and loved by God Himself, according to the example of Mary during her Visitation of her cousin Elizabeth: "The Lord has looked with favor upon His humble servant" (Lk 1:48).

Concrete act of conversion

We may not always be able to approach a priest for the purpose of making a confession, but we may at least be able to make a "review of our life" with a trustworthy friend. Thus, we shall put into practice for our greater good the advice of Saint James: "Confess your sins to one another and pray for one another in order that you may be purified" (Jas 5:16).

Prayer

Lord, do not quench the smoldering wick, have mercy on the poor sinner that I am, and grant me still to serve my brethren with a humble spirit. Amen.

Day 13

Wednesday of the Second Week of Lent

IN CHRIST, GOD HAS BECOME
A SERVANT

Scripture

Jesus said to the Twelve: "Whoever wishes to be first among you must be your servant....the Son of Man did not come to be served but rather to serve and to give his life as a ransom for many."

Matthew 20:27-28

Church Tradition

Saint Irenaeus of Lyons (2nd century): "How would man go to God if God had not come to man? How would man be freed from his mortal birth if he were not regenerated according to faith by means of a new birth given generously by God, thanks to the birth wrought of the Virgin's womb?" *Against Heresies*, IV, 33, 4

Brief meditation

How better to follow Christ in His humility, in His spirit of service, close to the poor and to the most rejected of the society? One path is to get close to His Mother who defined herself as "the humble servant" of the Lord (Lk 1:48). Since the rosary is a prayer of the poor—pray for us *poor sinners*—let us meditate on it often, asking Mary to conform our hearts to hers, in order better to be able to welcome her Son there.

Concrete act of conversion

Let us pray at least a decade of the rosary meditating on a mystery of the life of Christ especially suited to stimulating our desire to serve the needy and the misunderstood (they are often the same). For example, Gethsemane or Pentecost.

Prayer

Lord, if You need hands, here are mine. If You need blood, here is mine. If You need an ordinary and trusting servant, here I am! Amen.

Day 14

Thursday of the Second Week of Lent

ONLY GOD CAN KNOW US

Scripture

Thus says the Lord: "The heart is more deceitful than any other thing, and it is also perverse...

"I, the Lord, search the heart and probe the mind to reward all according to their conduct and as their deeds deserve."   *Jeremiah 17:9-10*

Church Tradition

Pope Francis (21st century): "As Pope Pius XII said, 'The greatest sin today is that men have lost the sense of sin.' Uriah [who was indirectly murdered by David] has become the symbol of all the victims of our tacit arrogance. When I see this injustice, this human arrogance and the danger that it may overtake me as well, the danger of losing the sense of sin, it does me good to think, in the name of Uriah, of all the victims of history who today also suffer because of Christian mediocrity, once we lose the sense of sin, once we give up the kingdom of God."   Homily in Rome, January 31, 2014

Brief meditation

If we were truly convinced that God alone can know us, uniquely in Him we would seek who we are and what we should do on earth. While one day a novice was explaining to Saint Jeanne Jugan how she would practice introspection to discover who she truly was, Jugan replied to her: "No, my daughter, may it suffice for you to ascend to Him and to immerse yourself entirely in Him!" (*Words of Saints*).

Concrete act of conversion

Have I also lost the sense of sin? Can I, for example, remember some grave faults that I have committed in my life? Did I not have the tendency to excuse them by whatever means in order to avoid accusing myself of them? Have I at least once confessed them to a priest with the firm purpose of committing them never again?

Prayer

Lord, You can do everything, and You know that I love You. Have mercy towards the sinner that I continue to be. May Your grace sustain me until the end of the journey! Amen.

Day 15
Friday of the Second Week of Lent

WHEN THE ONE EXCLUDED
BECOMES THE CORNERSTONE

Scripture

Jesus said to them: "Have you never read in the Scriptures: 'The stone that the builders rejected has become the cornerstone? (Ps 118:22)....Therefore, I tell you, the kingdom of God will be taken away from you and given to a people that will produce fruit in abundance.'"

Matthew 21:42a, 43

Church Tradition

Saint Peter, Pope and Martyr (1st century): "Come to Him [Christ], a living stone rejected by men, but chosen [and] precious before God. You, too, are like living stones, being built up into a spiritual temple (*oikos pneumatikos*) to form a holy priesthood to offer spiritual sacrifices acceptable to God through Jesus Christ."

1 Peter 2:4-5

Brief meditation

In today's biblical text, it is clearly said that a people truly faithful to the word of Christ should produce fruits worthy of His Kingdom. Saint Paul explains it when in his letter to the Galatians he enumerates the virtues that characterize "the heirs of God's Kingdom." For him,

these are not simply a matter of human quali-
ties, but authentic graces resulting from union
with Christ: "The fruit of the Spirit is love, joy,
peace, patience, kindness, generosity, faithful-
ness, gentleness, self-control" (Gal 5:22-23). If
therefore it is by the Spirit of Christ that we
live, then it is by the same Spirit that we put
the virtues into action. This holy life culmi-
nates in the faithful offering themselves as "a
living sacrifice, holy and acceptable to God"
(Rom 12:1).

Concrete act of conversion

Attend a Mass during the week and offer
yourself to God in a union of love with the Eucharistic offering of Christ made present on
the altar by the consecrated priest.

Prayer

*"Lord, You wanted neither sacrifice nor offer-
ing, but a body You fashioned for me.... Then I
said, 'Behold, I come, O God, to do your will!'"*

According to *Hebrews 10:5-7*

Day 16

Saturday of the Second Week of Lent

DIVINE LOVE GOES TO
MEET THE SINNER

Scripture

"The [prodigal and sinful] son set out for his Father's house...his father saw him and was filled with compassion (*esplagkhnisthê*)."

Luke 15:20

Church Tradition

Pseudo-Dionysius the Aeropagite (5th-6th centuries): "Is it not true that Christ draws near to those who turn away from Him, that He struggles with them, that He exhorts them not to despise His love, and that, if they show nothing other than disgust for Him and remain deaf to His appeals, He Himself becomes their advocate?"

Letters, To Demophilus (8)

Brief meditation

We are all prodigal sons and daughters in regard to the vocation of sanctity to which our Creator and common Father has called us since the beginning. "The God and Father of our Lord Jesus Christ...chose us in him, before the creation of the world, to be holy and blameless in his sight and to be filled with love"(Eph 1:3-4). Such a supernatural vocation, even if our nature had not been damaged originally, is not reachable to the unaided powers of a human creature. It is therefore necessary that God Himself should come to "seek out and save what was lost" (Lk 19:10). In this logic of love, we can maintain that it is already by a grace of the Father that the prodigal son had the inspiration to return, and the sign there-of is that the Father was looking towards the horizon and watching daily for the return of him who remained his beloved son despite his errors and faults. The lesson of this parable is that we could never seek out and find the heav-enly Father if first by His incarnate Word He did not *run* to meet us.

Concrete act of conversion

Let us try momentarily to put ourselves in the place of the prodigal son, exiled and bound by all kinds of harmful habits. Some of these might, after all, be our own. In his situation, what would we do? Would we have the cour-age and the faith to return to the Father and to confess to Him our miseries? But do we truly know them?

Prayer

Father, I have sinned against You and I have wounded myself by many sins. I am no longer worthy to be called Your child, but come to my aid by Your beloved Word. O Mary, our Mother, helpful to every repentant sinner, intercede for me and others like me, in order that we might through your Son go forward with great confi-dence to the Father! Amen.

Third Sunday of Lent

THE WORSHIPERS THAT GOD DESIRES

Scripture

Jesus said to the Samaritan woman: "But the hour is coming, indeed it is already here, when the true worshipers will worship the Father in Spirit and truth....God is Spirit, and those who worship him must worship in Spirit and truth."

John 4:23-24 (Year A)

Church Tradition

Saint Seraphim of Sarov (18th century): "It is in the acquisition of the Holy Spirit of God that lies the true goal of Christian life. Prayer, fasting, vigils, almsgiving, and all other good deeds are only the means for acquiring the Holy Spirit.... By 'the Kingdom of Heaven that is in you' [Lk 17:21], the Lord meant the grace of the Holy Spirit."

Interview with Motovilov, I & II, Sp. Orientale, no. 11

Brief meditation

It is good to say "I" in our prayers, because prayer does not aim at the dissolution of the self in a great undifferentiated "All." The "me" is not always a hateful, luring, and cunning bottomless pit. It can and must be freed from evil and reoriented to the Creator, its origin and destiny. This conversion is the work of the Spirit of Christ who works in all persons of good will, even if they have never heard anyone speak about Him (Mt 25:37). This conversion is best realized when the saving encounter occurs in the truth of the Gospel, believed and lived in the Church, and in the Holy Spirit, who makes the will of the Father to be perfectly accomplished (Rom 8:26). In the measure in which this work of salvation makes progress, personal prayer opens itself more and more to the dimension of the fraternal and universal "we." "My Father and our Father, my God and our God" (cf. Jn 20:17).

Concrete act of conversion

On this Sunday, let us try to meet a Samaritan, that is, a person who is a stranger to the Christian faith. Let us attempt to give him or her a little of our living water, that is, a brief testimony to the faith that makes us alive.

Prayer

Lord, I have nothing to draw the water of Your grace. Come to the aid of my meager faith and make me a witness of Your love. Amen.

Day 17

Monday of the Third Week of Lent

PROPHETS ARE SCARCE
AND UNHEEDED

Scripture

"If the prophet had told you to do something difficult, would you not have done it? How much more should you do it when he said, 'Wash and be made clean.' He went down and he bathed himself in the Jordan seven times as the man of God had instructed him to do. His skin became like the skin of a little child, and he was clean."   *2 Kings 5:13-14*

Church Tradition

Saint Vincent de Paul (16th-17th centuries): "It is a trick of the devil who deceives good souls by inciting them to do more than they really can, in order that they may do nothing at all. And the Spirit of God stirs us gently to do the good we reasonably can, in order that we may do it perseveringly and for the long haul."

Letter to Louise de Marillac, 1630

Brief meditation

Every prophet worthy of the name provides witness from their spiritual inspiration, while making sure to live constantly under the *discerning* and pastoral authority of their ecclesiastical or religious superior. While remaining subject to the Church, they make it their duty of telling the truth surpass all human prudence.

Do we know how to recognize among us such prophets? Some may be no more than wolves clothed in sheep's skin (Mt 7:15), but happily not all. We have personally known an authentic prophetic soul in the 1970s. Her name was Marthe Robin. This woman, inspired by and familiar with Calvary, preferred to say the least possible, since, she assured us, "We cannot give God to anyone except by radiating Him." In the preceding century, Saint Bernadette of Lourdes, whom some took then to be a living oracle, had the same approach as she warned: "God speaks to the heart without the noise of words." May God grant us such prophets today.

Concrete act of conversion

Can I come up with the names of at least three credible contemporary witnesses? After this, say a "Hail Mary" for each of them.

Prayer

"Holy Spirit, come into our hearts and send us from on high a ray of Your light.... To all believers who trust in You, give Your seven sacred gifts, give merit and virtue, final salvation and everlasting joy. Amen." Excerpt from *Veni Creator*

Day 18

Tuesday of the Third Week of Lent

PRAY EVEN IN THE FIRE OF TRIALS

Scripture

"Azariah then stood up, surrounded by flames, and said this prayer: 'Blessed are you and deserving of all praise, O Lord, the God of our fathers, and glorious is your name forever...

"For we, O Lord, have become the least of all nations, humiliated throughout the world in our day because of our sins.... Deliver us by your wonderful deeds, and let your name be glorified, O Lord."   *Daniel 3:25-26, 37, 43*

Church Tradition

Father Thomas Dehau, O.P. (19th century): "See the very young child. His language is no more than stammering, but how delightful it is to the heart of his mother. She herself becomes little again in order to babble with her child: they do not need anything else. What a striking image for what God is with His saints! If we could record their prayer in the midst of their trials, we would be astonished by their confident and candid simplicity. God suffices for them and—exquisite thing—the saints suffice for God. As it were, He forgets everything to listen to their loving babble, to get delightfully lost in it. How does what is happening around her matter to a mother when she is speaking to her child? Striking comparison. God forgets all the blasphemies, all the iniquities that would merit the disappearance of the earth. We wonder sometimes why God does not punish...Ah! The reason is that God is with His saints, very close to them. He forgets. He does not see. He does not hear anything else, and it is this babbling of the saints that wins us His mercy!" *As a Beggar*, 1993

Brief meditation

Azariah thought that it was the sins of his people that had brought misfortune upon him. Such a conviction comes to expression often in the Old Testament, but also in the New Testament: "The kingdom of God will be taken away from you and given to a people that will produce fruit in abundance" (Mt 21:43). "Jerusalem, you who kill the prophets and stone those sent to you.... Behold, your house will be abandoned and left desolate" (Mt 23:37-38). Closer to us the Virgin of Fatima clearly warns the nations: "If people do not cease offending God, in a short while there will occur another war worse than that one [of 1914-1918]" (apparition of July 13, 1917). That said, we must always recall that the prayer a single just person like Abraham can obtain forgiveness for an entire village (Gen 18:22-33), the intercession of one righteous person like Moses saves an entire people (Ex 17:11), and the confident supplication of even a great sinner like David secures a reduced punishment (2 Sam 24:17).

Concrete act of conversion

Since "all who want to live religiously in Christ will undergo persecution" (2 Tim 3:12), let us intercede on behalf of our possible future persecutors, according to the example of Father de Chergé who was assassinated in 1996 but who already since 1993 was asking God to have mercy on his eventual future murderer, "the friend of the last minute who will not have known what he was doing."

Prayer

"Father, forgive them, for they do not know what they are doing."   Luke 23:34

"Father, forgive them, for they do not know what they are doing."
— *Luke 23:34*

Day 19

Wednesday of the Third Week of Lent

EVERY WORD OF GOD
MUST BE CONSIDERED

Scripture

Jesus said to them: "Do not think that I have come to abolish the Law or the Prophets. I have come not to abolish but to fulfill them. Amen, I say to you, until heaven and earth pass away, not a single letter not even a tiny portion of a letter, will disappear from the Law until all things have been accomplished."

Matthew 5:17-18

Church Tradition

Saint Teresa of Ávila (16th century): "All the evil that comes upon this world derives from ignorance of the truths of Scripture of which not even the smallest point will fail to be realized." *Her Life Written by Herself*

Brief meditation

Many believers imagine that the Scriptures are ancient and pious stories, more or less historical, conveyors of teachings of great spiritual value, but scarcely more than this. They are, in fact, much more. The Sacred Scriptures are "another ciborium of God" (J.J. Olier). They contain in themselves not only essential truths concerning who is God, who is man, and what is his destiny, but also a unique "divine power"

(Rom 1:16), which in some people can accomplish conversions, healings, miracles, and exorcisms. Without the intervention of the Resurrected One, the Scriptures are no more than a dead letter, but with Him "the spirit is opened up" to their comprehension (Lk 24:45). They become a force of the living God in the service of all believers and unbelievers, the poor and suffering of the earth.

Concrete act of conversion

Let us resolve to read the Bible more often, especially those passages that the Roman liturgy proposes each day to the faithful. "Do you read the Bible?" asked Saint Augustine. "Then the Spouse speaks to you," he concluded.

Prayer

"Grant we pray, O Lord, that schooled through Lenten observance and nourished by your word, through holy restraint we may be devoted to you with all our heart and be ever united in prayer. Through our lord Jesus Christ, your Son, who lives and reigns with you in the unity of the Holy Spirit, one God, for ever and ever. Amen."

Collect of the Mass for the Wednesday
of the Third Week of Lent

Day 20
Thursday of the Third Week of Lent

JESUS, THE WAY TOWARDS
THE KINGDOM OF GOD

Scripture

"Jesus said to them: 'If it is by the finger of God that I cast out demons, then the kingdom of God has come to you....Whoever is not with me is against me, and whoever does not gather with me scatters.'"

Luke 11:20, 23

Church Tradition

Saint Benedict of Nursia (5th-6th centuries): "The one who will be host in the Lord's tent is the one who being tempted by the malignant devil casts him far from his heart's glance, reduces him to nothing, has seized his suggestions stirring in himself, and dashed them against (the rock that is) Christ."

Rule, prologue, 28

Brief meditation

In the book of Exodus (Ex 31:18), we see that the tablets of the Law are inscribed by the finger of God. Likewise, it is with His finger that Jesus writes on the dust in the presence of the accusers of the adulterous woman (Jn 8:6). The finger in question is the index finger, the one that goes with gestures of authority, of warning, of election, and even of condemnation. Traditionally, this finger is a symbol of the active presence of the Holy Spirit, who regularly goes together with Christ's exorcisms when He "rebukes the unclean spirit" (Lk 9:42). Throughout the Christian centuries, religious iconography has witnessed to this gesture of Christ, the victor over the forces of evil.

Concrete act of conversion

Get for yourself some holy water—every priest or deacon is happy to provide it upon request—and sign yourself with it at the beginning and conclusion of prayer. This water serves to connect us to our baptism by water and the Spirit.

Prayer

Lord, renew me in the saving waters of my baptism, cleanse me from all defilement, and protect me from every bad influence, visible and invisible. Amen.

Day 21
Friday of the Third Week of Lent

THE WHOLE LAW:
LOVE GOD AND NEIGHBOR

Scripture

Jesus said to the scribes: "Here is the first of all the commandments: 'Hear, O Israel, the Lord our God is the only Lord. Therefore, you shall love the Lord your God with all your heart, all your soul, all your spirit, and all your strength.' This is the first commandment, and the second is similar (*homoia*) to it: 'You shall love your neighbor as yourself.' There are no greater commandments than these."

Mark 12:29-31 (according to manuscripts A, W; cf. the parallel *Mt 22:39*)

Church Tradition

Saint Catherine of Siena (14th century): "If one loves Jesus from a pure and unselfish love, one loves also one's neighbor with the same love. As soon as a soul loves its Savior, it loves its neighbor, for the love of Christ and the love of neighbor are but one....The love one has for the latter proceeds from his divine love."

According to the *Dialogues*, chap. 64, 7

Brief meditation

Mysteriously, the universe reflects something of the infinite perfections of the Creator. It is, in any case, the affirmation of Scripture with regard to human beings: "Let us make man in our image and likeness" (Gen 1:26). Now, if as the Christian faith affirms that God is a Trinity of Persons (Mt 28:19) loving one another (1 Jn 4:16), it is *by love* that we have to be able to know better what man is and what God is. This knowledge can occur in the interior encounter with Christ's Spirit who joins our spirit (Rom 8:16) in order to make us love and pray as we should. If we were to summarize this in the light of the history of salvation what more should we say except that divine Love is essentially Gift (creator), Forgiveness (savior), and Communion (Spirit of love)?

Concrete act of conversion

What will I do concretely today to show my love of neighbor? In the coming weeks, what act of forgiveness and reconciliation will I do?

Prayer

"Lord, make me an instrument of Your peace. Where there is hate, let me sow Your love. Where there is injury, let me employ forgiveness. Where there is division, let me introduce unity. Where there is error, let me sow truth. Where there is doubt, let me propagate faith. Where there is despair, let me introduce hope. Where there is darkness, let me bring light. Where there is sadness, let me disseminate joy. Amen."

Prayer attributed to Saint Francis of Assisi

Day 22

Saturday of the Third Week of Lent

LOVE PRECEDES AND
EXCEEDS EVERYTHING

Scripture

The Lord declared to the House of Israel: "Your love (*chasdekhem*) is like morning mist, like the dew that goes early away.... For it is love (*chesed*) that I desire and not sacrifice, knowledge (*da'at*) of God rather than holocausts."

Hosea 6:4, 6

Church Tradition

Saint Angela of Foligno, T.O.S.F. (13th century): "Truly, there is no greater love on earth than the love that makes us cry over the sins of our neighbor.... The love that does this is not from this world."

The Book of A. of Foligno, Instruction no. 36, § 3

Brief meditation

In order to love better, a good way is to visit persons that are humble and that are completely given over to others. Authentic love radiates and is shared like smiling, without thinking about it. As regards the knowledge of God, it is not primarily about biblical or hagiographic reading. It is a gift from on high that comes from an act of faith in the omnipresent God and from an interior word that we address to Him with filial confidence: "Speak, Lord, your servant is listening."

Concrete act of conversion

Since today is Saturday, let us think about the Virgin Mary who followed Jesus so closely in all His mysteries. Let us ask her to help us to become better disciples, better brothers and sisters in the one communion of faith and love.

Prayer

"O Mary conceived without sin, pray for us sinners who have recourse to you. Amen."

Prayer entrusted by Our Lady to Saint
Catherine Labouré on November 27, 1830

Fourth Sunday of Lent

IN EVERYTHING, DISCERNING WHAT IS GOOD, JUST, AND TRUE

Scripture

Paul said to the Ephesians: "Once you were darkness, but now you are light in the Lord. Live as children of light, for light produces all goodness and righteousness and truth. Discern what the Lord finds pleasing. Take no part in the fruitless deeds of darkness, but rather seek to expose them." *Ephesians 5:8-11 (Year A)*

Church Tradition

Cardinal Charles Journet (20th century): "Because my heart is made for the totality of the Good, the Beautiful, and the True, because my heart is greater than the world, and because the world does not offer me more than partial goods (real or apparent), I can, in the presence of these goods, say 'yes' because they are *goods* or say 'no' because they are *partial.*"

Interviews about Grace

Brief meditation

Saint Paul explicitly calls Christians to discern in themselves and in their daily life, not so much the will of God—as if it were a decree written beforehand and to be approached as such—but what is pleasing to the Lord (Eph 5:10). This kind of discernment legitimates personal interpretation with its nuances and differences. Certainly, the divine Spirit suggests a direction and shows the horizon but rarely insists on a particular path over another. Of all the possible paths that the Spirit discloses to the faithful soul—let us not doubt it—the one that He prefers is not necessarily the most difficult or the most direct, the most famous or the most pious. It is the one that will allow this soul to use to the end (*eis telos* in Jn 13:1) its abilities to love and to be loved.

Concrete act of conversion

If I were to be asked to express in a single phrase my calling on this earth, what could I say? Would those close to me be surprised? Or, on the contrary, would they find that what I say corresponds sufficiently well to the reality that they know about me?

Prayer

"God, who enlightens everyone who comes into this world, illuminate our hearts with the splendor of Your grace, that we may always ponder what is worthy and pleasing to Your majesty and love You in all sincerity. Through Jesus Christ our Lord. Amen."

Prayer after Communion for the Fourth Sunday of Lent

Day 23

Monday of the Fourth Week of Lent

AFTER TRIALS, CONSOLATION

Scripture

"Sing praise to the Lord, O you his saints; give thanks to his holy name. For his anger lasts for only a moment, while his goodwill endures for a lifetime."

Psalm 30:5-6

Church Tradition

Saint Thérèse of the Child Jesus (19th century): "[Jesus, my Beloved,] recall that in the evening of Your agony, Your tears were mingled with Your blood. Dew of love, their infinite value caused the virginal flowers to sprout. An angel, showing You this chosen harvest, caused joy to be rekindled on Your blessed face."

Poems of Saint Thérèse, "Jesus, remember me"

Brief meditation

After the dark and violent storm, the clear and sometimes sunny weather returns. This is equally true in the spiritual life. Even during trials, the young Thérèse of the Child Jesus encouraged herself by singing: "No, nothing worries me, nothing can trouble me... above the clouds, the sky is always blue" (*Poems*, 52, 16-17). That said, for the disciple of Christ, there exists the possibility of true joy even within trials. Saint Paul testifies to this when he declares that he exults with joy in the midst of tribulations (2 Cor 7:4). Padre Pio testified to it equally to Father Agostino: "It is *at the same time* that the Lord burdens and relieves. While He imposes a cross, He gives you so much strength that in the simple fact of bearing this weight you find yourself simultaneously unburdened" (letter of December 15, 1917). It is this *felt* help of the strength of the Spirit that the Poor One of Assisi used to call "perfect joy" (cf. *Acts* 7, and *Little Flowers*, 8).

Concrete act of conversion

Let us consider testifying more to the joy that Christ left us as an inheritance, "That my joy may come to full measure in them" (Jn 17:13). This is for us also the heavenly counsel that Saint Joan of Arc heard in prison: "Be of good courage and have a cheerful face."

Prayer

"Lord, keep me from becoming an old grump. Allow me to retain a sense of humor that puts things, others, and even myself in their rightful place."

Father Joseph Folliet (20th century), excerpt

Day 24

Tuesday of the Fourth Week of Lent

JESUS VISITS ALSO
WHOEVER HAS NO ONE

Scripture

"Now in Jerusalem, by the Sheep Gate, there is a pool that in Hebrew is called Bethesda....A man who was there had been an invalid for thirty-eight years....Jesus said to him, 'Rise! Take up your mat and walk!' Immediately, the man was cured, and took up his mat and began to walk."
John 5:2, 5, 8-9

Church Tradition

Metropolitan Anthony Bloom (20th century): "A woman who for fourteen long years was in the habit of praying for some hours daily complained of never having had the feeling of the presence of God. When it was pointed out to her that she was talking all the time, she agreed to keep silent for some days. She became aware then that God was present, that the silence which surrounded her was not emptiness, but that it was inhabited [by God] and that the silent presence of God was making itself known to her by creating the same silence in her (1 Ki 19:12). She discovered then that prayer was being reborn in her quite naturally, but this was no longer the kind of discursive noise that had impeded God until then from making Himself known to her."

Living Prayer, "The Prayer of Silence"

Brief meditation

In the countryside, as today in the cities, more and more people suffer from loneliness. Although connected electronically to each other at every moment, they tolerate badly a deep relational vacuum that is not filled up by external activities. Those who are dearest to them are either far away or already in the great beyond. Thus, when these solitary individuals pray, they can adopt as their own the cry of the paralytic: "I have no one!" This is physically true, but it is not true spiritually. The communion of the saints in heaven and of the future saints on earth is not an empty word. There exists an invisible community of all the lonely faithful who trust in God and who pray for one another. This community of the poor, gathered mystically at the foot of the Cross, can offer much and can obtain much in the measure that they forget themselves to pray for those who are poorer and lonelier than they are.

Concrete act of conversion

If the world seems to be neglecting us rightly or wrongly, let us take this as an opportunity to help those less fortunate than we. Let us likewise consider giving affectionate attention to animals, flowers, and birds, for all of creation has been entrusted to human beings (Gen 1:28).

Prayer

"Open my eyes, Lord, to the wonders of Your love. I am the blind man on the roadside. Heal me. I want to see You! Amen."

Excerpt from hymn G79

Day 25

Wednesday of the Fourth Week of Lent

BETTER THAN A MOTHER,
THE LORD LOVES HIS CHILDREN

Scripture

"Break into song, O mountains...For the
Lord has comforted his people, and he will
show mercy to his afflicted ones.... Behold, I
have inscribed your name on the palms of my
hands."

Isaiah 49:13,16a

Church Tradition

Saint John Vianney, Parish Priest of Ars (19th
century): "God loves us more than the best of
fathers, more than the tenderest of mothers.
We have only to submit and abandon ourselves
to His will with the heart of a child."

Saint Parish Priest of Ars, His Thought, His Heart

Brief meditation

He who created the heart of the best parents,
such as the couple Louis and Zélie Martin, He
who "invented the Holy Virgin" (Saint Thérèse
of Lisieux, C.J., 31.8.10), the most merciful of
mothers, is the ineffable and holy Trinity, only
Source of all agape-love, of all unselfish affection. Knowing this and believing firmly, how
could we still fear to stray, especially if we
keep "our eyes fixed on Jesus, the leader of our
faith" (Heb 12:2)? And even if there should exist on the earth the heart of a father or mother

able to condemn us for having sinned too greatly, let us remain confident "for God is greater than our hearts!" (1 Jn 3:20).

Concrete act of conversion

If we are a mother or father, let us examine the way that we live out our parental mission. Do we live this beautiful vocation in a solely earthly way, without ever praying for our children, particularly never calling down upon them God's blessing in order that they may become fully happy and successful beings? Yes, even if this should mean great struggle and sacrifices for them and us?

Prayer

Ruach Adonai, divine Spirit [of feminine gender in Hebrew], take us maternally under Your protecting wing; come make us more similar to the Son of God, in order that, in Him and in You, we may love perfectly our heavenly Father from whom comes every good thing. Amen.

Day 26

Thursday of the Fourth Week of Lent

THE SCRIPTURES ALSO BEAR WITNESS

Scripture

Jesus said to them: "Search the Scriptures carefully because you believe that through them you will gain eternal life....If you truly believed Moses, you would have believed in me, for it is about me that he wrote. But since you do not believe what he wrote, how will you believe what I say?"   *John 5:39, 46-47*

Church Tradition

Saint Augustine of Hippo (4th-5th centuries): "The Bible has a low entry way, but it is high and spacious for the one who agrees to make progress in it. It rises by degrees, all the while remaining veiled in mystery.... My pride despised its simplicity, and I did not penetrate its depths. I despised being little, while believing myself to be great."   *Confessions*, III, 5

Brief meditation

With Lent, we live a time of retreat and grace in order to know and love better the invisible God Who gives meaning to everything. As we thus make ourselves more familiar with the supernatural world, new struggles emerge. We must first fight daily against our carnal passions (1 Pet 2:11), but also against the evil spirits that, like roaring lions, prowl around "looking for someone to devour" (1 Pet 5:8). Let us take advantage of this time of testing to imitate the Lord in His own battle. As He did, let us use "the sword of the Spirit, which is the Word of God" (Eph 6:17): "Depart from me, Satan. It is written..." (Mt 4:10).

Concrete act of conversion

Let us often read the Holy Scriptures in order to prevent in us the loss of the sense of truth, the sense of the divine, and the taste for beautiful and good things. Let us go further: may we learn by heart some verses that speak to our heart. Thus, thanks to our memory, employed often, we shall have a spiritual treasure to use in every moment, including and especially in times of trial and sorrow.

Prayer

Lord Jesus, I want to love You with all my heart, all my soul, all my strength. I want to keep all Your words so that Your Father and You may come to me with Your mutual Spirit and make me Your dwelling. Amen.

According to *John 14:23*

Day 27
Friday of the Fourth Week of Lent

THE SECRETS OF GOD
REMAIN HIDDEN TO THE IMPIOUS

Scripture

"Such was their reasoning, but they were wrong, for their own malice blinded them. They did not discern the hidden plans of God, or hope for the recompense of holiness or recognize the reward destined for innocent souls."

Wisdom 2:21-22

Church Tradition

Father Bernard Bro, O.P. (20th century): "Evil is the absence of that which allows a being to be fully himself...In man, it is able also to put up resistance to the attraction of that which is better. The human person can say 'no.' He may prefer to revert to a lesser good."

Love and You Will Know Everything

Brief meditation

Unbelievers are not all impious, bad persons with a hard heart and obtuse spirit. Far from it! The separation between the lambs and wolves does occur not principally at the level of a profession of faith or of atheism, but on the basis of the individual conscience of each person. Whoever acts fraternally towards others is already in the movement of Christ (cf. Mt 25:40). Whoever proclaims himself to be a disciple of the invisible God but does not love his brother whom he sees is, according to St. John, "a liar" and the good spirit "is not in him" (1 Jn 2:4). How do we recognize the presence of the good spirit? It never distances itself from Christ, His commandments, or prayer. On the other hand, the evil spirit is the companion to trouble, impatience, anger, self-love, smugness, and indifference towards what is not oneself or for oneself. The evil spirit incites us to follow idols and earthly happiness, never the Christ of the beatitudes.

Concrete act of conversion

Let us often ask the Holy Virgin to protect us from the evil angels and evil influences. Let us follow this advice of the Parish Priest of Ars who knew about devilish persecution: "If you invoke her when you are tempted, this Mother so full of tenderness will come quickly to your aid."

Prayer

Lord, command this evil spirit that assails me with evil thoughts and say to it as You did once the storm: "Quiet! Be still!" (Mk 4:39). O Immaculate Mary, as once when evil voices arose from the torrential river (Feb. 19, 1858, according to J.-B. Estrade), throw a severe glance upon the menacing spirits and make them permanently quiet. Amen.

Day 28

Saturday of the Fourth Week of Lent

LORD, I HAVE ENTRUSTED
TO YOU MY CAUSE

Scripture

"Jeremiah prayed thus to the Lord: 'I was aware of this O Lord, because you had made it known to me, then you revealed to me their evil deeds. I had been like a trusting lamb that was being led to the slaughter....O Lord of hosts, you who judge righteously and test the heart and the mind, allow me to behold your vengeance on them, for to you I have committed my cause.'"

Jeremiah 11:18-20

Church Tradition

Saint Gertrude of Helfta (13th century): [In a vision, Christ said to Gertrude:] "The more they blame without just cause your conduct, the more My Heart will give you testimonies of My love, because that will make you completely similar to Me, whose actions they were pleased to misinterpret."

The Herald of the Divine Love, book IV, ch. 58

Brief meditation

Our judgments concerning others are more often negative than positive, often marked by severity than by generosity. However, Jesus warned strongly that the measure we use to measure others will be used equally for us (Mt 7:2). Regardless, we forget, and we pour out on others vinegar or venom without almost noticing it. Victims of slander or calumny can hardly assert their rights, since it all happens behind their back. Often the victim can do no more than place themself in the hands of the just Judge, the Providence that watches ceaselessly over the humble and the suffering. This explains why the ancients insisted more on mastery over the tongue than on mastery over the flesh, advising that mastery over words led habitually to better mastery over all the bodily senses.

Concrete act of conversion

Let us attempt to listen twice as much as we speak. During a deep dialogue with someone, let us make sure to do 50/50. If we are in great shape and full of ourselves, we are at risk of doing 80/20, almost not even listening, but insisting that our interlocutor hardly has anything to teach us, whereas we have so much to say to them!

Prayer

"Speak, Lord, for Your servant is listening."

1 Samuel 3:9

"Then Mary said to the angel: 'Behold the handmaid of the Lord. May it be done to me according to Your word!'" *Luke 1:38*

Fifth Sunday of Lent

BY LOVE, LEARNING TO DETACH
ONESELF FROM ONE'S LIFE

Scripture

Jesus said to his disciples: "The hour has come for the Son of Man to be glorified. Amen, amen ...unless a grain of wheat falls into the earth and dies, it remains just a grain of wheat. However, if it dies, it bears much fruit....If anyone wishes to serve me, he must follow me... If anyone serves me, my Father will honor that person."

John 12:23-26 (Year B)

Church Tradition

Saint Thérèse of the Child Jesus (19th century): "Well do souls say, 'But I do not have the strength to accomplish so great a sacrifice.' Let them therefore do what I did: put forth a great effort. The good God never refuses this first grace that supplies the courage to act. Thereafter, the heart is strengthened, and we go from victory to victory."

Final Interviews, CJ, 8.8.3

Brief meditation

To become independent and completely responsible for one's actions is one of the noble goals of all education. By love, being ready to reject this independence, often won by a hard fight, is one of the fruits of every affective and spiritual life. Indeed, human freedom achieves all its meaning and dignity in the act of love that leads it to deny itself, partially or completely, so as to exist no longer by and for itself alone, but by and for another. To attain to such detachment is less the fruit of ascetic effort than it is an act of wild trust. By love, one detaches oneself from one's possessive me in order to go towards the other, and ultimately towards the totally Other. Then beings emerge truly free because they are moved exclusively by Love, beings who can truly say with Saint Paul: "It is no longer I who live, but Christ who lives in me!" (Gal 2:20).

Concrete act of conversion

It is easier to lose oneself momentarily, believing then to be in complete self-renunciation, than it is to find oneself humbly in the merciful gaze of Christ from the height of the Cross or in the gaze of the Father in the very moment of our creation. Confidently, let us try to unite, in their mutual Spirit, these two gazes that are but one.

Prayer

"Who are You, O my very gentle God, and who am I, poor worm and Your humble servant?"

Prayer of Saint Francis of Assisi on Mount Alvernia

Day 29

Monday of the Fifth Week of Lent

JESUS FORGIVES AND
SAVES THE SINNER

Scripture

[All the accusers of the adulterous woman] went away one by one.... Jesus said to her: "Woman, where are they? Has no one condemned you?" She replied: "No one, sir." "Neither do I condemn you," Jesus said. "Go on your way, and sin no more." *John 8:9-11*

Church Tradition

Saint Thérèse of the Child Jesus (19th century): "Yes, so that love may be fully satisfied, it is necessary that it lower itself to nothingness and that it transform this nothingness into fire. O Jesus, I know, one does not pay for love, except by love!" *The Story of a Soul, 223*

Brief meditation

People have often asked themselves what Jesus could have written on the dust of the ground. The act itself was not trivial, since the Jewish tradition taught that to write in the dust did not violate the Sabbath and consequently the sacredness of a venerated place. With Jerome, the Fathers of the Church thought that Jesus wrote down every grave sin of all the accusers who were present. More likely, according to what Jesus himself declared in the same chapter, "I judge no one" (Jn 8:15), he wrote down some extenuating considerations: the absence of her partner, the legal requirement of two or three witnesses (Deut 17:6), the impossibility of carrying out a capital sentence the same day as the condemnation (Mishna, Sanh. 4:1). In any case, the important thing is that by inviting first those "without sin" to respond, He forced them gently, by His finger pointed to the dust, a symbol of man (Ps 103:14), to discover themselves as sinners and therefore unworthy of judging their neighbor.

Concrete act of conversion

Jesus does not dispute that the woman had sinned in a certain moment. He only refuses to imprison her definitively in her sin. The forgiveness of the Just One opens a space of freedom that allows the sinner to choose freely to change her conduct. And we ourselves, do we not need to convert from some hidden sin, a harmful habit, a toxic relationship?

Prayer

"We pray O Lord, that we may be constantly cleansed of our faults by [your grace], and by following Christ hasten our steps toward you."
Communion Prayer, Monday of the Fifth Week of Lent

Day 30
Tuesday of the Fifth Week of Lent

BEING FROM ON HIGH OR
BEING FROM BELOW

Scripture

Jesus said to the Jews: "You belong to what is below, whereas I belong to what is above. You belong to this world, but I am not of this world....When you have lifted up the Son of Man, then you will know that I AM [*egō eimi*], that I do nothing on my own authority and I say nothing except what the Father has taught me." *John 8:23, 28*

Church Tradition

Blaise Pascal (17th century): "Outside of Jesus Christ, we do not know what is our life, our death, God, or ourselves." *Thoughts, frag. 548*

Brief meditation

The lifting up of the incarnate Son of God unto the cross is an essential moment of the *salvation* of the world, but equally of the *revelation* of what is truly and concretely the love of God for His creatures. In the Gospel of John, Golgotha is the ultimate Sinai, a privileged place of trinitarian epiphany: there the Father glorifies the Son (Jn 8:54), there the Son glorifies His Father (Jn 17:1), and there too is their mutual Spirit who is already mysteriously transmitted (*paredōken to pneuma*) to humanity awaiting divinization (Jn 19:30; 2 Pet 1:4).

At each Mass, this revelatory and salvific moment is realized before the faithful, who are then invited, according to the grace proper to each, to unite themselves with the single offering of Christ, Savior and Lord.

Concrete act of conversion

Offering oneself to God, by and in Christ, can remain relatively theoretical if concrete gestures of love towards our neighbor do not accompany our prayer. Have we thought of donating some of our blood?

Prayer

O Father, "grant that we, who are nourished by the Body and Blood of Your Son and filled with his Holy Spirit may become one body, one spirit in Christ. May He make of us an eternal offering to You, so that we may obtain an inheritance with Your elect.... May this Sacrifice of our reconciliation, we pray, O Lord, advance the peace and salvation of all the world."

Excerpts from Eucharistic Prayer III

Day 31

Wednesday of the Fifth Week in Lent

IT IS THE TRUTH THAT SETS US FREE

Scripture

Then Jesus said to those Jews who believed in him, "If you remain faithful to my word, you will truly be my disciples. You will know the truth and the truth will set you free".... "Amen, amen, I say to you, everyone who sins is a slave of sin....Therefore, if the Son sets you free, you then will truly be free."   *John 8:31-32, 34, 36*

Church Tradition

Catechism of the Catholic Church (20th century): "The grace of Christ is not in the slightest way a rival of our freedom.... On the contrary, as Christian experience attests especially in prayer, the more docile we are to the promptings of grace, the more we grow in inner freedom and confidence during trials, such as those we face in the pressures and constraints of the outer world. By the working of grace, the Holy Spirit educates us in spiritual freedom in order to make us free collaborators in His work in the Church and in the world."

Part Three, Life in Christ, § 1742

Brief meditation

It is certain that the truth sets us free, but it is not alone in bringing about this salutary effect. A selfless life focused on others also produces internal freedom. Moreover, Jesus affirms that pure hearts will see God (Mt 5:8); now, the purity that turns away from sin, which makes everything dark, is itself productive of spiritual freedom. And ultimately what is true freedom if not the real and concrete capacity of each person to act according to what one discerns in oneself to be best, what a clear conscience dictates, what the light breeze of the Spirit suggests? Thus, the freest beings are all in some manner *prophets*, because they are carried along by an authentic divine Wind. It was the same Spirit that once impelled towards the Temple and up close to Jesus the two righteous persons, Simeon and Anna (cf. Lk 2:27, 38).

Concrete act of conversion

Today's gospel is clear: it is the truth to which the Son testifies that sets us free and makes us strong. Therefore, let us try to give more attention to our spiritual life *with Christ* and *in His Spirit*: let us read more often His Word in the Scriptures and the trustworthy lives of His friends and witnesses, for example, *Come Be My Light: The Private Writings* by Mother Teresa.

Prayer

"Almighty and merciful God, graciously keep from us all adversity, so that, unhindered in mind and body, we may pursue in freedom of heart the things that are yours. Through our Lord Jesus Christ, your Son, … Amen."

Roman Missal, Collect for the Thirty-Second
Sunday of Ordinary Time

Day 32

Thursday of the Fifth Week of Lent

JESUS TRANSCENDS ALL TIMES

Scripture

Jesus said to the Jews: "Your father Abraham rejoiced that he would see my day. He saw it and was glad....Amen, amen, I say to you, before Abraham was, I AM [*egō eimi*]."

John 8:56, 58

Church Tradition

Catechism of the Catholic Church (20th century): "Everything in Jesus' life was a sign of His mystery. His deeds, miracles, and words all revealed that 'in Him the whole fullness of deity dwells bodily' (Col 2:9). His humanity appeared as 'sacrament,' that is, the sign and instrument, of His divinity and of the salvation He brings: what was visible in His earthly life leads to the invisible mystery of His divine sonship and redemptive mission."

Part One, The Profession of Faith, § 515

Brief meditation

"Abraham would see my day," declares Jesus. How should we understand this strange remark? It is possible that during his lifetime Abraham had a prophetic vision of his future King and Savior (Gen 22:17) or that in the abode of the dead he received the grace of being able to encounter Christ in prayer such as Moses and Elijah would experience on Mount

Tabor (Lk 9:30). This detail of the Gospel of John suggests that, even if Jesus was historically present in His earthly flesh in the first century of our era, His human soul assumed by the divine Word could at any time come to visit in a spiritual and mysterious manner other epochs. For Him, this was probably not so much a jump back to the past or forward to the future as much as a temporary erasure of time for the glorious emergence into history of the divine eternity in which are included all times of history. The matter is as difficult to believe as it is to explain. The fact remains that the Church has known some rare mystics who have claimed to have been transported to the time of Jesus and to have been seen by Him in the course of an historical event recounted in the gospels. The "I AM" of Jesus dwells mysteriously in every time, and the Eucharistic realization of His offering on the cross is a consequence thereof, acknowledged and believed by all Catholic and Orthodox Christians of the whole world.

Concrete act of conversion

Let us meditate for a moment on the non-necessity of our having been created: we could never have existed or never have been born. It is possible that we could never have known the risen Christ, nor have met Him in Himself or in His friends. Let us repeat with Clare of Assisi the prayer of thanksgiving that she uttered while dying, "May You be blessed, my Lord, Who have created me!" (Cel 28, 46).

Prayer

"O God, Who are beyond all, what appellation can name You, what hymn can sing of You? You alone are ineffable. You alone are unknowable. All beings celebrate You, all pay You homage. The whole universe raises to You a hymn of silence. You are the destiny of all. Have mercy, O You Who are beyond all!"

Saint Gregory of Nazianzus, P.G., 37, 507-508, excerpt

"This is my Son, my Chosen One. Listen to him."
— *Luke 9:35*

Day 33

Friday of the Fifth Week of Lent

THE UNITY OF LOVE OF
THE FATHER AND THE SON

Scripture

Jesus said to the Jews: "If I am preforming the works of my Father, then do not believe me. However, if I am doing them, then even if you do not believe me, at least believe my works, so that you may realize and understand that the Father is in me and I am in the Father."

John 10:37-38

Church Tradition

Catechism of the Catholic Church (20th century): "Christ's whole earthly life—His words and deeds, His silences and sufferings, indeed His manner of being and speaking—is *Revelation* of the Father. Jesus can say: 'Whoever has seen me has seen the Father,' (Jn 14:9) and the Father can say: 'This is my Son, my Chosen One; listen to him!' (Lk 9:35). Because our Lord became man in order to do His Father's will (cf. Heb 10:5-7), even the least characteristics of His mysteries manifest 'God's love... among us'" (1 Jn 4:9).   Part One, The Profession of Faith, § 516

Brief meditation

It is not easy to grasp that the Father and His Word are at once similar and different just as the heart of the sun is neither its brightness nor its heat while being part of one and the same sun. Painters have sometimes tried to represent the Father and the Son sitting in heaven. Most often, the Father appears as a noble old man enthroned on the left or above His Child. Some rare painters constitute the exception and manifest a theology more subtle and respectful of the mystery. An example of this is the icon of the *Trinity* by the Russian monk Andrei Rublev that depicts the encounter of Abraham with God Himself in the form of three men or angels (Gen 18:1-33). We may also point to another example in *The Crowning of the Virgin* by Enguerrand Quarton (15th century). The artist dares to represent the Father and the Son like two twin kings, side by side, linked to each other by a dove symbolizing the Holy Spirit. Whether in the work of Rublev or Quarton, we do not perceive any special precedence between the persons.

Concrete act of conversion

By the help of a search engine, for example, let us look at the trinitarian paintings of Rublev and Quarton and let us meditate on them in silence for some minutes.

Prayer

"O my God, Trinity Whom I adore, help me to forget myself completely so as to be set firmly upon You, immoveable and peaceful, as if my soul were already in eternity. Amen."

Hymn of Saint Elizabeth of the Trinity
(19th century), excerpt

Day 34
Saturday of the Fifth Week of Lent

REUNITING THE SCATTERED
CHILDREN OF GOD

Scripture

The high priest Caiaphas said to the San-
hedrin: "You do not seem to realize that it is
better for us that one man die for the people
rather than the whole nation be destroyed...as
the high priest that year he was prophesying
that Jesus was to die for the nation, and not
for the nation alone, but to gather into one the
dispersed children of God."   *John 11:49-52*

Church Tradition

Saint John Paul II (20th century): "Prayer is
the 'soul' of ecumenical renewal and of the
yearning for unity.... Ecumenical dialogue is
not simply an exchange of ideas. In some way,
it is always an *exchange of gifts*."

Encyclical *Ut unum sint*, May 25, 1995, § 28

Brief meditation

It is a beautiful and great thing to be able
to have, in the same Church, spiritual unity
in the same Creed and in the same hope under the leadership of the same pastor. Jesus
Himself yearned for the unity of His own by
and in the Spirit: "May they be one as We are
one.... That the love with which You loved me
may be in them and I in them" (Jn 17:22-23, 26).
Alas, human beings are fickle and conflicted,

often incapable of submitting themselves unswervingly to any authority of earth or heaven. Already at the time of the first Christian community, when "believers had all things in common" (Acts 2:44), Saint Paul remarked nonetheless: "Among you there are divisions" (1 Cor 11:18). The children of God sometimes find themselves more divided and scattered than the children of the sinful world (Mt 12:26; Lk 16:8). Human beings have so much trouble accepting that the other thinks differently than we. Let us ask the Holy Spirit to bring about a communion of love among us that transcends all differences without necessarily erasing them all.

Concrete act of conversion

Every year, in the third week of January, all the Christian churches celebrate the Week of Unity. If you have not participated in this time of prayer and ecumenical dialogue, decide to do so next year, and, try to have a peaceful exchange with a separated brother or sister.

Prayer

"Lord Jesus, grant us all to meet one another in You. May Your prayer for the unity of all Christians rise up from our souls and our lips. May this unity be as You will and by the means You will. May You, who are perfect charity, grant us to find the way to genuine communion in obedience to Your love and truth. Amen."

According to Father Paul Couturier,
"Prayer for the Unity of Christians," excerpt

Sunday of the Palms and the Passion

IF THEY KEEP SILENT,
THE STONES WILL CRY OUT

Scripture

"Then they brought the colt to Jesus, and after spreading their cloaks over the colt, they helped Jesus to mount it...the entire multitude of his disciples began to praise God joyfully for all the mighty works they had seen him perform, proclaiming: 'Blessed is the king who comes in the name of the Lord'...[Jesus answered the Pharisees:] 'I tell you, if they keep silent, the stones will cry out.'"

Luke 19:35-40 (Year C)

Church Tradition

Vatican Council II (20th century): "Let Christians walk in wisdom in the face of those outside, 'in the Holy Spirit, in genuine love, in the word of truth' (2 Cor 6:6-7), and let them be about their task of spreading the light of life with all confidence and apostolic courage, even to the shedding of their blood."

Dignitatis humanae, § 14

Brief meditation

Every Christian who wants to follow Christ more closely exposes himself not only to the risk of tribulations (2 Tim 3:12), but also to the duty of witnessing to the faith (Mk 16:15). Charles de Foucauld used to remark that the Spirit of Christ could not inspire us to stay quietly in the fold with a few faithful sheep when most of the others were wandering alone in the mountains. It is not a matter of our wanting to seduce them by means of beautiful words or of convincing them with solid demonstrations, but only of our confession of faith *at the right moment*, briefly, and simply our faith in the One Who impels us to believe beyond what is visible (Heb 11:27) and to love beyond what is reasonable (1 Cor 4:10). In this, we shall follow the example of the great missionary St. John Paul II, who loved to repeat: "Let us propose, without imposing!" (September 10, 2000).

Concrete act of conversion

The question is not when I made my last sacramental confession, but when I made my last missionary confession. Have I recently had the courage to speak a little about my faith to those close to me who have meager faith or are indifferent? Recall Joseph of Arimathea after the death of Christ. "Taking courage (*tolmōsas*), he went to Pilate and asked for the body of Jesus" (Mk 15:43).

Prayer

O Lord, if You need a donkey to take You as far as Jerusalem, here I am! If You need a megaphone to announce You to Your friends and Your enemies, here I am! If You need a Simon of Cyrene to help You on the hard way, here I am! If You need a thief of good will and equally as weak as he was, here I am! In Your pains and in Your Kingdom, remember me, Lord!

Day 35

Monday of Holy Week

THE CHOSEN ONE OF GOD DOES NOT QUENCH THE SMOLDERING WICK

Scripture

"Here is my servant whom I uphold, my chosen one in whom my soul delights. I have put my Spirit upon him; he will establish justice among the nations....He will not break a bruised reed, nor will he snuff out a smoldering wick; faithfully he will establish justice."

Isaiah 42:1-3

Church Tradition

Saint Augustine of Hippo (4th-5th centuries): "Because the truth has made you free, may love make you a servant!"

Commentary on Psalm 90, sermon 2, 11

Brief meditation

From the biblical point of view, what is a servant of God? Always a humble person among the humble (*anawim*), a blessed one of the Lord, "meek and lowly, taking refuge in His name"(Zep 3:12), a righteous person belonging to the remnant of Israel "who does no wrong and tells no lies"(*ibid.*, v. 13). Jesus places Himself squarely in this line of the humble ones of Israel when He designates Himself as the One who serves (cf. Lk 22:27) and whose heart is meek and humble (cf. Mt 11:29). This perfect model of servants knows how far to humble

Himself to save "what was lost" (Lk 19:10) such that He never overwhelms the sinner but seeks him out against all contrary circumstances. Jesus said to the adulterous woman: "Neither do I condemn you" (Jn 8:11). Are we convinced that God never wants the death of the sinner (cf. Ezek 33:11), but only his salvation, the real salvation that endures eternally?

Concrete act of conversion

Without fixating, let us question our memory. What are the offenses that we have suffered in the past that continue to hurt us? Will we forgive our persecutors for good, for example, by praying for them and rejecting any thought of revenge, or will we forgive only superficially so as merely to have a clear conscience?

Prayer

Lord, now that You are in Your Kingdom, remember me. May Your saving power deliver me from all evil, so that I may dwell forever in the paradise of Your Heart. Amen.   (cf. Lk 23:43)

Day 36

Tuesday of Holy Week

THE GREAT TRIAL MAKES
US MORE FRAGILE

Scripture

Simon Peter asked Jesus: "Lord, where are you going?"..."Where I am going, you cannot follow me now, but you will follow me later on." Peter said, "Lord, why can I not follow you now? I will lay down my life for you. ... Will you really lay down your life for me? Amen, amen, I say to you, before the cock crows, you will have denied me three times." *John 13:36-38*

Church Tradition

Pope Benedict XVI (20th-21st centuries): "Evil has power via man's freedom, whereby it creates structures for itself. For there are quite obviously structures of evil. They eventually exert pressures on man; they can even block his freedom and thereby erect a wall against God's penetration into the world. God did not conquer evil in Christ in the sense that evil could no longer tempt man's freedom; rather, he offered to take us by the hand and to lead us. But he does not compel us."

The Salt of the Earth

Brief meditation

An ardent faith and a generous love should not make us forget the human fragility that moved Christ to say: "The spirit is willing, but the flesh is weak" (Mt 26:41). Even contemplatives, even confessors of the faith, even saints can know moments of failure. This is the meaning of the oft-cited proverb: "The just man falls [at least] seven times, then he rises" (Prov 24:16). With humor and realism, the Parisian Carmelite friar, Lawrence of the Resurrection (17th century), used to declare when he breached the Rule: "Basically, I am not surprised, because I know myself well. Rather, what surprises me is when I do not fall." Let us have the same humility, without of course excusing ourselves too easily or exempting ourselves from all effort at conversion or penance.

Concrete act of conversion

Let us consider our recent mistakes and weaknesses. Let us ask pardon for them from God. Then let us take advantage of this Holy Week to confess them to a priest. Let us then make a few practical resolutions that we need to stay on the right course.

Prayer

Lord, I believe; nevertheless, come to the aid of my meager faith!   cf. *Mark 9:24*

Day 37

Wednesday of Holy Week

NOT FLEEING IN THE FACE OF TRIAL

Scripture

"I have not rebelled, I have not turned away. I offered my back to those who struck me, my cheeks to those who plucked my beard. I did not shield my face from insults and spitting. The Lord God is my help; therefore I have not been disgraced. Rather, I have set my face like flint, knowing that I will not be put to shame."

Isaiah 50:5-7

Church Tradition

Saint Thérèse of the Child Jesus (19th century): "When the blue sky becomes dark and seems to leave me, my joy is to stay in the shade, to hide, to lower myself. My joy is the holy will of Jesus, my only love. Thus, I live without fear. I love both the night and the day. My joy is to remain small. Also, when I fall on the way, I can get up quickly, and Jesus takes me by the hand." *Poems of Saint Thérèse,* "My Joy"

Brief meditation

It is prudent to protect oneself from declared or surreptitious enemies, as Scripture itself encourages us to do: "Be on your guard, for people will hand you over to courts and scourge you" (Mt 10:17). If despite all precautions, we are struck by the violent, before any possible response, it is wise to ask them the reason for their action, as did Christ during His Passion after He was slapped by the servant of the high priest: "If I have spoken wrongly, testify to the wrong; but if I have spoken rightly, why do you strike me?" (Jn 18:23). Certainly, Jesus preached love and forgiveness for one's enemies (cf. Mt 5:44), exhorting us "not to resist the wicked" (Mt 5:39), but He also asked His disciples to be "as clever (*phronimoi*) as serpents and as innocent (*akeraioi*) as doves" (Mt 10:16). Christian non-violence is not cowardice in the face of evil or stoic indifference. To protect the common good, Christian non-violence can sometimes employ certain forms of proportionate dissuasion, as Jesus Himself suggested on the eve of His Passion: "But now, if you do not have a sword, sell your cloak and purchase one!" (Lk 22:36).

Concrete act of conversion

Constantly in the dark hours, the sins of our enemies assail us, wound us, and cause us to despair. Let us try to look at them from the balcony of the sky. Let us ponder in these hostile brothers and sisters only what we shall admire in them throughout eternity.

Prayer

Lord, grant me the grace of patient charity. With the strength of Your Spirit, may my love forgive everything, believe everything, hope everything, endure everything.

cf. *1 Corinthians 13:7*

Day 38

Holy Thursday

DAY OF PURIFICATION
AND COMMUNION

Scripture

Jesus said to Simon Peter: "Anyone who has bathed has no need to wash further, except for his feet, for he is clean all over. You also are clean, although not every one of you is clean."

John 13:10

"Whenever you eat this bread and drink this cup, you proclaim the death of the Lord until he comes."

1 Cor 11:26

Church Tradition

Saint John Paul II (20th century): "The Church and the world have a great need of eucharistic worship. Jesus waits for us in this sacrament of love. Let us be generous with our time in going to meet Him in adoration and in contemplation that is full of faith and ready to make reparation for the great faults and crimes of the world. May our adoration never cease."

Letter *Dominicae cenae* (*Lord's Supper*) to all
bishops, Vatican, February 24, 1980, I, 3

Brief meditation

The Eucharist is a spiritually invigorating, *Christ-vivifying*, food if we leave room for the One who comes into us with all His love and forgiveness. But how can He dwell, "I with him and he with Me" (Rev 3:20) if our heart has not previously rejected firmly all anger towards our neighbor and all attachment to sin? May our hatred for our neighbor, and therefore for ourselves, not cast Him out! Before every reception of communion, let us have the courage to forgive, and He will willingly forgive us in turn (cf. Mt 6:14). Then let us receive Him with faith and respect, knowing how to give Him time, attention, and affection by silent and fervent adoration.

Concrete act of conversion

Holy Thursday is an eminently Eucharistic day. Let us take advantage of the prayer vigil that will be held in a nearby parish in order to give Christ who is sacramentally present "at least one hour" (Mk 14:37).

Prayer

"Almighty God, just as we are renewed by the Supper of Your Son, so may we enjoy his banquet for all eternity. Amen."

Communion Prayer, Holy Thursday

Day 39

Good Friday

THE IMMOLATION OF
THE LAMB OF GOD

Scripture

"He was despised and shunned by others, a man of sorrows who was no stranger to suffering. We loathed him and regarded him as of no account,... Although it was our afflictions that he bore, our sufferings that he endured, we thought of him as stricken, as struck down by God and afflicted. But he was pierced for our offenses and crushed for our iniquity; the punishment that made us whole fell upon him and by his bruises we have been healed."

Isaiah 53:3-5

"When Jesus had taken the wine, he said, "It is finished." Then he bowed his head and gave up his spirit."   *John 19:30*

Church Tradition

Mother Yvonne-Beloved of Jesus, Augustinian (20th century): "The greatest moment in the history of the world was the crucifixion of the Savior. That moment is made present by the Mass. Above our sinful earth, chalice and paten are always raised."   *Spiritual Writings*

Father Thomas Dehau, O.P. (19th century): "The only way to stand when the cross comes is to do so with Mary and in Mary."

The Compassion of the Holy Virgin

Brief meditation

The words of the dying, bearers of their ultimate thoughts, should rouse our attention more. Often uttered in pain, they can express truths about life and its mystery. On Good Friday, let us listen again to the seven last words of our Savior: 1. "Father, forgive them, for they do not know what they are doing" (Lk 23:34); 2. "Amen, I say to you, today you will be with Me in Paradise" (Lk 23:43); 3. "Woman, behold your son;… behold your mother" (Jn 19:26-27); 4. "My God, my God, why have you forsaken Me?" (Mt 27:46; cf. Ps 22:2); 5. "I thirst" (Jn 19:28; cf. Ps 69:22); 6. "It is finished" (Jn 19:30); 7. "Father, into Your hands I commend My spirit" (Lk 23:46; cf. Ps 31:6).

Concrete act of conversion

Let us try to get to a nearby parish to meditate on the Way of the Cross. We can also listen to a Christian radio station at 3 p.m. if we cannot attend church services. It would be good to mark this day not only with a fast from food, as the Church invites us to do, but also with a time of silence.

Prayer

"May abundant blessings, O Lord, descend upon us who have honored the death of Your Son in the hope of our own resurrection; grant us pardon and consolation, increase our faith, and ensure our eternal redemption. Amen."

According to the final prayer of the Mass of Good Friday

Day 40

Holy Saturday

SILENCE, RECOLLECTION, HOPE

Scripture

"Now there was a good and upright man named Joseph who was a member of the council....He took down the body of Jesus, wrapped it in a linen shroud, and laid him in a tomb.... On the Sabbath they rested in obedience to the commandment."

Luke 23:50, 53, 56b

Church Tradition

Thomas à Kempis (14th-15th centuries): "If you do not know how to meditate on heavenly things, direct your thoughts to Christ's passion and willingly behold His sacred wounds. There you will find great comfort in suffering."

The Imitation of Jesus Christ, Book II, 1, 4

Chiara Lubich (20th century): "Mary! Death is made beautiful by the knowledge that beyond the shoreline of life there is a Mother—and what a Mother!—who waits for us. The mystery of death, which often frightens and depresses us, becomes clear, welcoming, and sweet."

Spiritual Writings

Brief meditation

It is in consideration of the ever-fervent Christian faith of Mary on the day of Holy Saturday, while the rest of the world had ceased to believe (cf. Mk 16:14), that Saturday was chosen by the Church as the ultimate Marian day.

Now, Saturday prepares and anticipates Sunday, as Mary, the new Eve, prepares and anticipates humanity saved and glorified in Jesus, the new Adam, the firstborn from the dead, at once true God and true man. Through her compassion at the foot of the Cross (cf. Jn 19:25) and her ever-living faith even during the great absence of Holy Saturday, Mary has merited to become the Mother of the Church and therefore the Mother of each of us and firstly of the Apostle John (cf. Jn 19:27).

Concrete act of conversion

This Holy Saturday is a day of great liturgical silence, but also of strong hope and fervent prayer, Let us pray in union with the Immaculate Virgin and, if the Spirit moves us to it, let us renew our personal relationship with her by, for example, making use of an act of consecration like that of Saint Louis-Marie Grignion de Montfort.

Prayer

"O Mother of all men and women, and of all peoples, with the love of the Mother and Handmaid of the Lord, embrace this human world of ours, which we entrust and consecrate to you, for we are full of concern for the earthly and eternal destiny of individuals and peoples.... Let there be revealed, once more, in the history of the world the infinite saving power of merciful Love!"

Consecration of the World to Our Lady,
Saint John Paul II, March 25, 1984, excerpt

Day 1 of the New Time

Easter Sunday

STRIVING FOR THE REALITIES
THAT ARE ABOVE

Scripture

Behold, [the risen] Jesus met the women [Mary Magdalene and Mary, the mother of James] on their way and greeted them…."They approached him, embraced his feet, and worshiped him. Then Jesus said to them, 'Do not be fearful. Go and tell my brethren to go to Galilee. There they will see me.'"

Matthew 28:9-10
Col 3:1-2

Church Tradition

Patriarch Athenagoras (19th century): "The Resurrection is the beginning of the transfiguration of the universe."

Recurrent idea in his preaching

Pope Benedict XVI (20th-21st centuries): "Christianity is always the mustard seed and the tree at the same time, always simultaneously Good Friday and Easter…. What we need are people inwardly seized by Christianity, who experience it as joy and hope, who are true loving souls. These people we call saints."

The Salt of the Earth

Brief meditation

During this Lent we were renewed in the grace of this important liturgical time, but our earthly pilgrimage continues. Let us experience it every day with a pure heart, an open mind, and a joyful soul pervaded by the Holy Spirit. Let us keep our "gaze fixed on Jesus" (Heb 12:2), the Risen One Who precedes us into Galilee (Mt 26:32), that is to say, Who awaits us in Paradise, our true homeland. In the last times, He will return to us, descend gloriously to earth to restore everything in Himself, and take us to the Father (cf. 1 Thes 4:17). So today, on this holy Easter Day, it is also timely to say with the whole Church, as after each consecration, "Come, Lord Jesus!" (Rev 22:20).

Concrete act of conversion

Among the Jewish people, it is customary to invite to the Passover meal family and close friends and to leave an empty place also for the prophet Elijah, just in case the Lord allows him to attend as a surprise guest. Let us be inspired by this beautiful example of faith and charity, and let us consider inviting to our Easter meal some lonely person, one of the *anawim* of the Lord.

Prayer

"On this day of Easter, God our Father, You make accessible to us eternal life by the victory of Your Son over death, and we celebrate His resurrection. May Your Spirit make of us new men and women so that we might rise with Christ in the light of life."

According to the Entrance Antiphon for Easter Sunday

CONCLUSION

As a conclusion and an act of thanksgiving, we invite the reader to pray with us the beginning of Psalm 34, which is so often employed in the liturgies of Eastertime.

I will bless the Lord at all times;
   his praise will be continually on my lips.
My soul will glory in the Lord;
   let the lowly hear and be glad.
Magnify the Lord with me;
   let us exalt his name together.

I sought the Lord, and he answered me;
   he set me free from all my fears.
Look to him and you will be radiant;
   your faces will never be covered with shame.
In my anguish I cried out;
   the Lord heard my plea,
   and I was saved from all my troubles.

The angel of the Lord encamps around those
     who fear God,
   and he delivers them.
Taste and see that the Lord is good;
   blessed is the one who takes refuge in him.

Ps 34: 2-9

The Five Sorrowful Mysteries

(Said on Tuesdays and Fridays throughout the year, and daily from Ash Wednesday until Easter Sunday)

The Sorrowful Mysteries recall to our mind the mysterious events surrounding Christ's sacrifice of His life in order that sinful humanity might be reconciled with God.

1. The Agony in the Garden - Mt 26:36-46

JESUS, in the Garden of Gethsemane, You suffered a bitter agony because of our sins; grant me *true contrition.*

2. The Scourging at the Pillar - Mt 27:26

JESUS, You endured a cruel scourging and Your flesh was torn by heavy blows; help me to have the *virtue of purity.*

3. The Crowning with Thorns - Mt 27:27-31

JESUS, You patiently endured the pain from the crown of sharp thorns that was forced upon Your head; grant me the strength to have *moral courage.*

4. The Carrying of the Cross - Mt 27:32

JESUS, You willingly carried Your Cross for love of Your Father and all people; grant me the *virtue of patience.*

5. The Crucifixion - Mt 27:33-50; Jn 19:17-30

JESUS, for love of me You endured three hours of torture on the Cross and gave up Your spirit; grant me the grace of *final perseverance.*

FROM THE CROSS TO THE EMPTY TOMB

Most Rev. Arthur J. Serratelli, S.T.D., S.S.L., D.D.

The author invites you to journey with those who were with Jesus in His last hours. You may be like Peter one day, and like Judas, Simon, Mary Magdalene, or Our Lady on another. This Lenten book provides a deeper appreciation for God's eternal saving love. 96 pages. Size 4³⁄₈ x 6³⁄₄.

No. 928/04—Flexible cover **$6.95**
ISBN 978-1-947070-13-4

JESUS' LAST DAYS

Most Rev. Arthur J. Serratelli, S.T.D., S.S.L., D.D.

Through Bishop Serratelli's reflections on the similar accounts of the four evangelists, we re-live Jesus' Passion bathed in the light of Easter glory. We will appreciate how the Cross remains the instrument of our salvation and see more clearly our own call to discipleship. 128 pages. Size 5 x 7.

No. 932/04 – Flexible cover
ISBN 978-1-947070-35-6 .... **$6.95**

catholicbookpublishing.com

THROUGH HIS WOUNDS WE ARE HEALED

— by Vojtěch Kodet, O. Carm. This brief but profound book helps us to more fully understand how the Way of the Cross can be a wonderful means of uniting ourselves and the difficulties in our lives more intimately with Christ and His sufferings. 64 pages. Size 4 x 6¼.

No. 116/04—Flexible cover..........**$4.95**
ISBN 978-0-89942-116-2

MY POCKET WAY OF THE CROSS

— by St. Alphonsus Liguori. With glorious full-color illustrations, this pocket- or purse-size book offers those who wish to pray the Stations a handy companion for this popular devotion on the Sacred Passion of Our Lord. 48 pages. Size 2½ x 3¾.

No. 18/04—Flexible cover **$1.50**
ISBN 978-1-937913-30-4

UPLIFTING THOUGHTS FOR EVERY DAY

— by Rev. John Catoir. We can eliminate negative thinking and improve our emotional life by filling our mind with uplifting thoughts. 192 pages. Size 4 x 6¼.

No. 197/19—Dura-Lux cover.........**$9.95**
ISBN 978-1-937913-02-1

THE IMITATION OF CHRIST

— by Thomas à Kempis. Prayer book size edition. This treasured book has brought peace to readers for many ages by showing how to follow the life of Christ to which all are called. Includes a full-color Rosary and Stations of the Cross section. 288 pages. Size 4 x 6¼.

No. 320/19—Dura-Lux cover **$12.95**
ISBN 978-1-941243-16-9

NEW CATHOLIC BIBLE
Giant Type Edition

This faithful, reader-friendly translation includes the complete Old and New Testaments in easy-to-read type; notes are at the end of each book. The NCB is intended to be used by Catholics for daily prayer and meditation, as well as private devotion and group study. Easy-to-use 6½ x 9¼ format. 2480 pages.

No. 617/19BG – Dura-Lux cover
ISBN 978-1-947070-40-0 .... **$55.95**

ST. JOSEPH EDITION
NEW CATHOLIC BIBLE
NEW TESTAMENT AND PSALMS

We are pleased to offer our popular NCB New Testament and Psalms together in one volume in four different bindings.

Both texts are complete and their best features remain: readability; plentiful, insightful, and informative footnotes; helpful cross-references; 36 two-color illustrations; and the words of Christ in red.

This text is intended for use by Catholics in daily prayer and meditation, private devotion, and/or group study. 1232 pages. Size 4⅜ x 6¾.

No. 647/19GN – Dura-Lux cover
ISBN 978-1-941243-92-3 .... **$17.95**

St. Joseph NCB NEW TESTAMENT

This easily understandable study edition with large, easy-to-read typeface features complete notes and references, self-explaining maps, a handy Study Guide, lists of the Miracles and Principal Parables of Jesus, a Liturgical Index of the Sunday Gospels, a Bible Dictionary, the words of Christ in red type, and over 30 photographs. Ideal for schools and Bible study. Gilded edges. 528 pages. Size 6½ x 9¼.

No. 311/19 – Dura-Lux cover
ISBN 978-1-947070-66-0 .... **$17.95**

catholicbookpublishing.com